Exploring a theme: Puzzling Questions

Exploring and responding to puzzling questions lies at the heart of religion. What is the purpose of life? What happens when people die? Why do bad things happen to good people? If God made the world, who made God?

> I've been asking these questions
> For days and days.
> My mind is in
> A question maze!

This is how nine-year-old Sophia expresses it in her wonderful poem 'I wonder' on p.25.

These, and questions like them, arise naturally out of the subject matter of religious education. Developing activities that encourage children to ask and respond to such deeper questions is the bread and butter of the subject. Questioning is also at the heart of all good learning and teaching. The Primary strategy in England highlights its importance. Not only does the strategy identify the importance of teachers developing their own questioning skills, in order to challenge and deepen children's thinking, but most importantly, it stresses the value of enabling children to reflect on and pose their own questions. This is an area in which RE leads the way.

This publication brings together some practical strategies for stimulating pupil's questions and responses, along with some guidance for teachers on professional issues relating to the challenges involved. Try some of the strategies and be amazed at what children are capable of.

Joyce Mackley (Editor)

RE Today weblink: www.retoday.org.uk

This series introduces a new service for subscribers. The RE Today website will provide some free additional resources and classroom ready materials. Look out for the 'Re Today on the web' logo at the end of selected articles.

... ess can be found in each ... azine.

Engaging with 'big' questions: planning, questioning and responding to children's questions

When she was five, Vera Navratil looked up into the night sky of Montevideo and asked her mother, 'Do the dead go to heaven?'

'Yes.'

'And when God dies, what heaven does he go to? Does he go to a special heaven higher up?'

On the same night in Ribero Preto, many leagues north of Montevideo, Marcos Awad, who was the same age as Vera, was looking at those very same stars. Marcos asked his mother, 'Who made us?'

'We were made by God.'

'And God?'

'And God what?'

'Who made him?'

'Nobody made God. God made himself.'

'But what about his back? How did God manage to make his back?'

*By **Eduardo Galeano**, translated by Mark Fried © Eduardo Galeano.*

Have you ever been asked or thought about these or similar questions? It's very likely that you have. There are many different types of questions. These are quite profound. They cannot be answered simply or easily. They cannot be looked up on the internet!

These questions, or questions like them, have probably existed as long as human beings have existed. They are deep questions about meaning and purpose. They are at the heart of the religious teachings of the world. They are central to effective and engaging RE!

In England, the **eight-level scale in the QCA non-statutory Framework for RE** identifies progression in the skill of asking and responding to questions.

• Most six-year-olds (L1) should be able to talk about things which puzzle them and make them wonder;

• at seven, most should be able to ask and respond sensitively to questions (L2);

• by the time they are eleven, most pupils should be raising and suggesting answers to questions and issues raised by religion and belief (L4).

The planned use of focused key questions by teachers is a key factor in raising pupils' achievement and enjoyment in RE.

There are three main ways in which questions can be used to improve learning in RE:

1. **In planning** – using questions to focus and structure RE teaching and learning;

2. **In teacher questioning** – the planned use of probing questions to deepen and extend children's thinking and responding;

3. **By the children themselves** – the planned used of learning activities to enable children to ask and respond to deeper questions.

Planning RE

When planning RE units across the key stage: use a key question as the unit title rather than a thematic title.

For example, instead of using a title such as 'Special Books', aim for a deeper conceptual understanding by asking *What makes some books sacred, what do they tell us and how are they used?*

Or instead of a unit simply titled 'Jesus', sharpen and deepen the learning by focusing on exploration of a question such as *Who was Jesus and why do people follow him today?'*

Teacher questioning – the use of probing questions

Teacher questioning is a critical skill. It is the most usual form of interaction between the teacher and the pupil. Learning will be improved if you develop your questioning technique to ensure that you are providing appropriate challenge.

Review the types of questions you most often use in RE. Which of the following do you use most?

Descriptive: What? When? Where? Who? How?

Reflective: How did it feel? What did it make you wonder? Why?

Speculative: What if...? What might happen next? What might the person be thinking? What question might they ask? What would you/ Jesus/Muhammad/Guru Nanak do?

If you find that many of your questions fall into the 'descriptive', plan some probing questions which encourage reflection and speculation.

For example: When exploring prayer ask: 'If you were God what prayers would you answer?' After reading the story about Jesus in the Temple, ask 'Is getting angry always a bad thing?' When exploring religious holy days: 'What do you think a Christian or Muslim might say if asked the difference between a holiday and a Holy Day?

Developing children's own skills of questioning and responding

Move away from tasks which limit children to safe factual recall. Use learning activities that encourage children to explore some of the big or 'ultimate' questions. Such activities should enable pupils to

• think more deeply

• reflect on and express their own questions, ideas and feelings

• listen and respond sensitively and respectfully to each other as well as to the teacher

• suggest how someone from a faith perspective might respond to a 'big' question

• begin to realise that some questions are difficult to answer and that there may not be agreement about what the right and wrong answers are.

Skilful questioning – sentence stems for the teacher

Can you match the skill words in the box to the bubbles?

Which types of questions do you use most?

Which types of questions will help you increase the challenge of tasks and raise pupils' achievement?

What was the main idea...?

Who was the key character...?

Can you explain in your own words...?

What is the difference between...?

Can you name...?

Can you describe what happened when..?

Can you tell me why...?

What happened after...?

Can you apply this to some experience of your own...?

What might happen if you/someone put this into practice today? Why?

What questions would you ask of...?

What is the turning point/key moment? Why do you say this?

How is this similar to...different from...?

Can you explain what must have happened when...?

What were some of the motives behind...?

Can you devise your own way to...?

What would happen if...?

What are the main ingredients of...? (e.g. worship)

What is ..like and why?

What do you think about...?

Do you think ... is a good or a bad thing? Why do you think this?

Is there something you can't make your mind up about? What are the reasons for and against?

What is the value of....? Why?

How is...feeling?

What do you think...is wondering?

What might...do next/decide?

How would you feel if...?

What is the meaning of...?

Why do you think ...do, say, believe...?

Can you think of another meaning for this?

What did this make you think about in your own life?

What did it make you wonder?

What do you think matters most to...? Why is it so important to them?

What matters to you? How do you show this?

Skill Words

reflection analysis interpretation application synthesis
empathy understanding evaluation knowledge

Responding to tricky questions in RE

RE is all about setting tasks and activities which encourage children to engage with 'big' questions, yet understandably teachers can feel nervous of opening up questions that they might find difficult to respond to. If you steer clear of exploring ideas (and inevitably questions!) about such things as endings, death, God, what lies beyond, good and evil, you miss the heart out of RE, for such issues really are the bread and butter of the subject, and at the heart of pupils' spiritual development. Rather than sticking to 'safe' territory, venture out into the unknown, but take some tips with you!

Tips

- Keep responses open to keep children pondering.

- Use 'owning and grounding' language; 'in my opinion' or 'some Hindus' would say...'

- Be honest in your response – but always let children know that there are a range of views and beliefs.

- Establish ground rules with the class for discussing controversial issues.

- Be sensitive to family beliefs and values. Encourage children to ask the questions at home as well.

Some examples

A child asks...	A response might be..........
Who borned God? (six-year-old)	Encourage a 'let's explore this together' approach, e.g. 'That's a good question...and I wish I knew the answer to it... *What do you think?*'
Did Nana go to heaven when she died? (five-year-old)	Respect possible family sensitivities and beliefs. Aim to keep the child pondering and avoid giving closed answers, e.g. '*Some people would say so.... What does mummy or daddy say?.... Often people who follow a religion believe in heaven.... What do you think?*'
Do you believe in God?	This is the sort of question that often makes teachers feel personally exposed or worried about overly influencing young children, but it is important to be honest. Couch your reply with – '*but not everyone believes /thinks this*'. Suggest asking other adults in school as well to show that there is a range of responses.
How do you know the Bible isn't made up? (eight-year-old)	You could say: '*People have different views. Some believe the Bible is the word of God, others do not.... We could ask some people. Who could we ask?*' Encourage a 'let's explore this together' approach. Again, aim to keep the child pondering and avoid closed answers. Questions of truth are central to RE. It is important to help children to see that there are different forms of truth – that for some the message of a story might be true even if the details are made up (as with a 'moral' in a favourite fiction book); but for others what a sacred text says is literally true because it is believed to be from God.
Why do people believe that – I think it's stupid!' (nine-year-old)	Remind children that such comments can cause upset to other people – that it's important to try to understand why it is important to someone else and to express points of view in a non-offensive way. Throw questions back, e.g. 'How would you feel if someone said what you think is 'stupid?'

Persona dolls and RE: developing children's questions and answers about people of faith in the Foundation Stage

The Persona dolls strategy has been developed as a non-threatening and enjoyable way to raise equality issues and counter racism with young children. It can also be an invaluable tool for religious education. Using Persona dolls for teaching and learning about people of faith is a very effective way of engaging children with views, beliefs and ideas that may be different to their own. It encourages them to ask questions and think through perspectives that may be new to them. Ideally meeting real people of faith is preferred, but as this is not always feasible, using Persona dolls makes quality teaching and learning easily available to all.

07.04.2006

Preparation

- It is best to have a designated time for using Persona dolls, preferably weekly. The end of the morning session or the beginning of an afternoon, when children might be more 'open' to sitting and being reflective, is ideal. Regular weekly sessions enable children to know what's expected and to be able to recall information about the personas readily. As with all learning it is useful to keep revisiting the issues under discussion for several sessions so that learning can become embedded.

- Gather as for a usual 'carpet time' either in a cluster or circle. The practitioner needs to be sitting on a chair with the doll sitting on his/her lap.

- Use one Persona doll at a time to support current learning. Practitioners need to know well the details of what the persona likes, thinks and believes. Good preparation is essential. *The Little Book of Persona Dolls* includes clear outlines for Christian, Sikh, Hindu, Jewish and Muslim personas.

Meeting Samuel and Yusuf

Here we will look at Jewish and Muslim personas and how they can be used for effective learning in religious education in the Foundation Stage.

Context

- Children may be looking at an RE topic from the local Agreed Syllabus such as 'Our Special Objects' or 'Times of Celebration'. A Persona doll may be integrated into the unit, perhaps replacing or complementing a faith visitor, a picture book, or DVD clip.

- It is important to remember that some children in the group may have no understanding of what it is to have a faith and so practitioners will need to work slowly and surely to help them to realise what it means. Others may have a very clear understanding of their own faith and be reluctant to find about another, so extra sensitivity will be required.

A typical Persona doll session

Session outline

Start with a 3–4-minute introduction of the Persona doll by asking some questions and revisiting some earlier learning. Questioning which stimulates discussion needs to be planned for carefully. It is a good idea to have a number of explicitly set questions that are intended to promote participation.

Example 1: Introducing Yusuf

- Do you remember who this is? [They always do!]

- Can you describe what Yusuf believes about Allah? [That Allah created the world and is to be prayed to every day]

- This week Yusuf is going to share with you how he prays. [Show a prayer mat, a picture or a real one]

- Before he prays he has a good wash. Why do you think Yusuf does this? [Allow ideas to flow!]

- Are there times when YOU have a good wash?

- What do you think Yusuf is thinking while he is praying? [Any ideas are relevant to help their understanding]

- What do you think he feels when he prays?

- Are there any questions you would like to ask Yusuf? [You may not need to ask this as children may already be asking lots of questions!]

Allow as many children as possible an opportunity to respond: often they repeat what has gone before, but just as often have their own special insights.

Finish on a positive note: 'You have learned so much about Yusuf and why he prays – well done.'

The important learning in this session is that regular prayer is very important to Muslims. This idea needs to be repeated until children really understand its importance.

Yusuf – who he is, what he likes, thinks and believes

Before introducing Yusuf to the children you will need to know about Yusuf's Persona. You may need to share some of these details with the group or they may be peripheral to the discussion. They can be 'released' over several sessions throughout the year.

- Yusuf is five years old. He has an older sister called Safiyya.

- He goes to school in the daytime and a special school in the evening held at the Mosque. This is the building where Muslims worship Allah, who has 100 names to describe how wonderful he is.

- Here Yusuf learns to read Arabic so that he knows more about Allah by reading the Qur'an, the Muslim Holy Book.

- Yusuf prays every day to Allah and uses a prayer mat like the rest of his family.

- The most important time in Yusuf's family's year is the time of Ramadan and the celebration of Eid. Eid falls at the end of Ramadan. Ramadan is a month of praying and fasting when Muslims pray to be better people.

- At Eid, Yusuf celebrates by wearing new clothes, giving and getting presents and eating special food.

Questions that encourage understanding of Yusuf's beliefs

How could we find out what a Mosque and a prayer mat look like?

Do you have a special book that you like to read?

Do you think it would be hard to learn another language like Arabic?

Do you know another language?

What do you find it hard to learn?

What is the most important time for Yusuf and his family?

Do you have special times of the year when you celebrate with your family?

Example 2: Introducing Samuel – who he is, what he likes, thinks and believes

- Samuel has a young sister, Rachel.

- His mum and dad take them to the synagogue each week to pray to God.

- They have special ceremonies on the eve of the Shabbat (Saturday, the Jewish Holy Day) where their mum prepares a special meal, lights a candle and prays to God.

- The best days of Samuel's year are the lively spring festival of Purim, the harvest festival Sukkot and the winter festival of Hanukkah.

- Samuel's family eat specially prepared food called 'kosher' food.

4-5

It is important to keep a record of the details of the doll's 'story'. The doll's record should contain such things as name, age, gender, family, religion, likes and dislikes, place of worship, holy book, foods and festivals. You will need to share some of these details with the group immediately; others can be 'released' over several sessions throughout the year.

Questions that could be asked to encourage understanding of Samuel's beliefs

'Family' is very important to Jewish people. When his grandparents come to visit they make sure that Samuel is learning about Jewish things.

- What do your family ask you when you have 'get-togethers'?

- Do you have a time when all your relations come to your home?

Samuel's grandparents want to know about how he enjoys the synagogue on the Sabbath (Saturdays) and what he does in Sabbath school. He learns stories about Joseph and his multicoloured coat, which he tells his family (Genesis 37-47) and lots of other stories from the Torah, the Jewish Holy book.

- Do you have any stories that your family like to share?

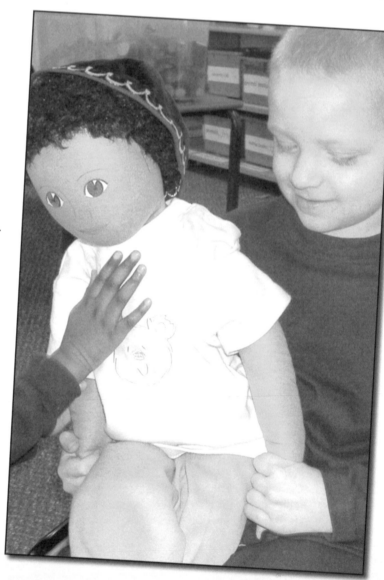

Links to Foundation Stage Profile targets

Social Development 7: Understands that people have different needs, views, cultures and beliefs which need to be treated with respect.

Social Development 8: Understands that s/he can expect others to treat her or his needs, views, cultures and beliefs with respect.

Emotional Development 5: Has a developing awareness of own needs, views and feelings and is sensitive to the needs, views and feelings of others.

Emotional Development 6: Has a developing respect for own culture and beliefs and those of other people.

Language for Communication and Thinking 1: Listens and responds.

Language for Communication and Thinking 4: Listens with enjoyment to stories, songs, rhymes and poems, sustains attentive listening and responds with relevant comments, questions and actions.

Knowledge and Understanding of the World 6: Finds out about past and present events in own life, and in those of family members and other people s/he knows. Begins to know about own culture and beliefs and those of other people.

See also

The Little Book of Persona Dolls by Marilyn Bowles, Featherstone Education, 2003, ISBN 1 904187 86 2

To purchase religious Persona dolls:

The Parrotfish Company,
51, North Street,
Maldon,
Essex,
CM9 5HJ

Tel/fax 01473 655007

www.parrotfish.co.uk/persona_dolls.htm

A website with video clips illustrating use of Persona dolls: www.blss.portsmouth.sch.uk/earlyears/eypdolls_tr.shtml

Exploring puzzling questions: two practical activities for 5–7-year-olds

For the teacher

Good RE for younger children

- recognises, values and encourages children's capacity to wonder at and enjoy aspects of their experience;
- recognises and takes seriously children's questions and ideas about profound, puzzling or difficult areas of life.

Good learning for younger pupils will start from the children, be fun, be tactile. It always a good idea to use a stimulus to get children involved. This might be a faith story, an artefact, a picture or a visitor.

Using a Story: Stop, Think, Question, Share

Overview: by focusing on a key character in a faith story, this activity encourages children to see through the eyes of another person. It uses speaking and listening skills and stimulates children's questions.

Teacher preparation: Make sure you are clear about the key religious idea in the faith story. In RE it is important to engage children in exploring the key religious idea within a faith story. Make sure that you are clear about what this is. Avoid watering down meanings into the purely social, emotional and moral. Young children can begin to grasp key concepts in religious stories, for example the concept of promise in the Noah story or good overcoming evil in the Divali story, if they are introduced to them in a way that links to their own experience.

Procedure

Tell the story. Talk about the story. Ask children to suggest what they think the story means. Ask children to pick out a key moment. Retell the story – *stop* at the key moment. Choose one character.

Think: Provide children with four focus questions

What is he doing?

How is he feeling?

What puzzles him? What question might he ask?

If you could be there, what question would you ask?

Share: In turns each child shares their answers with a partner.

Record: Children could draw the character and write the questions they think he asked in speech bubbles. Puzzling questions from the story could be gathered onto a 'Puzzling Questions' board.

Example: The story of Moses and the Burning Bush

Questions children thought Moses might ask:

Why don't you get burned up?

Why have you picked me?

I'm frightened...who will help me?

Questions they would ask if they were there:

Why did you take your shoes off?

What will you do?

Using a picture: describe and draw

Overview

Using pictures, photographs or drawings, this activity allows children to see through the eyes of another person. It teaches the importance of speaking and listening carefully, and stimulates children's questions.

Procedure

Ask children to work in pairs. Give everyone one picture and some drawing materials. Tell the children not to show their picture to their partner.

One partner describes his or her picture to the other, who has to try to draw it from the description alone. After five minutes, the pair reverse roles. Because of the time limit and age of the children, the drawings will be quite simple. The important element is the describing, not the drawing.

The participants then take it in turns to compare their drawings with the original pictures. Ask them if anything important was left out? What? Why?

Follow-up questions

What do you think the picture shows?

What are the people doing?

What do you think is happening? Why do you say this (what clues have you seen for this?)

Imagine you can put yourself in the picture. You can ask someone a question. Who would you ask and what would you ask them?

5-7

I can...

The following pupil-friendly criteria could be used to assess children's responses to this activity.

To what extent *can pupils*:

- use correct vocabulary (angel; God) to talk about what the picture shows (L1);

- ask a thoughtful question to do with the picture.

Pupils working at L2 may also be able to:

- use religious words and phrases to identify a Jewish or Christian belief connected with the picture;

- talk about what the angel stands for and ask some questions about God and angels.

Example

The picture below will spark some interesting responses from children. It is the primary sector winner of the 2005 Spirited Arts competition and can be downloaded from the Spirited Arts gallery on the PcfRE website:

www.pcfre.org.uk/spiritedarts/art05/whereisgod/wig8.php

This drawing may be copied for use in class.

This is a line drawing of a picture by Lewis Kay, aged 7, of Brinsworth Manor Infant School. (A colour version is on the back cover and on the PcfRE website at www.pcfre.org.uk)

Lewis said this about his picture:

'Talking to God is like talking to a friend. Sometimes God sends angels to speak to people like in the Christmas Story. And sometimes God sends the ladder so people can go up to Heaven. The angels help Him a lot.'

Godly Play: engaging young children in religious story

For the teacher

- Godly Play is a method that uses artefacts and models to explore children's innate spirituality – originally used in church contexts, now adapted as an exciting innovative tool which can be used to support an RE lesson.

- Its aim is to build a community and enable children and adults to step into a sacred space and wonder together.

- Each Godly Play lesson follows the pattern of the Christian Eucharist. The main steps are

- gathering the community

- unfolding the religious story

- asking the 'wondering' questions in a time of reflection

- creative work based on the story

- a plenary or sharing of ideas when some children share and others listen

- the 'Feast' (a basket of raisins is easy to administer!)

- the 'sending out' (to play, lunch or home time).

See also

Godly Play: www.godlyplay.org.uk

Jerome W Berryman, *The Complete Guide to Godly Play Volume Two* (BRF 2003, ISBN 1-889108-96-0).

Expectations

The activities described here were assessed against the following criteria (based on the local Agreed Syllabus, drawing on the non-statutory National Framework for RE).

Can children:

- use religious words and phrases to identify some features of the story of The Exodus and its importance for some people? (L2 Attainment Target 2)

- respond sensitively to questions about their own and others' experiences and feelings? (L2 AT2)

- identify the impact that religion has on people's lives? (L3 AT1)

- make links between their own and others' experiences? (L3 AT2)

Using Godly Play to explore the Judaeo-Christian story of the Exodus

Lizzie McWhirter, RE and Spiritual Development Officer for Coventry Diocese, writes:

I visited two Voluntary Controlled Primary schools in Warwickshire, Wolston St Margarets and Salford Priors, to see what the children's reactions would be. In one school, I worked with two very different Year One and Two parallel classes. In the other, I worked with a pure Reception class and a pure Year One class. Some of the children had behavioural problems. Godly Play, however, is a great strategy, and has the ability to draw all children in to engage with the story.

The following pages describe the activities and the children's responses.

The lesson

The gathering

Children gathered in a circle around a space which contains the Foundation Stage sand tray, which for the purpose of the lesson had been transformed into a desert box!!

The story is unfolded

Using simple wooden figures with no faces to represent Moses, Miriam and the People Of God, I told the story of the Exodus slowly with plenty of space for reflection. I then sat back and asked the Godly Play wondering questions.

The wondering questions (and children's responses)

I wonder which is your favourite part of the story?

Samuel: When Moses told the people to put the blood of the lamb on their doorstep so the eldest son would not get killed by the angel of death.

Tia: When Pharaoh said the people can go – if they stayed for ever they would have to do the things he said for ever.

Callum: When Moses and God came together and when the sea was torn apart.

Robbie: Doing somersaults through the water like being a gymnast.

I wonder which is the most important part of the story – and is it the same as your favourite part?

Sam: The most important part of the story was when Moses saved the family of God because otherwise they would have been captured for ever and might even die there.

Daniel: When God helped the people get over the river.

Tom: When the king told them that they couldn't leave and then he told them they could leave.

Amelia: When Moses came close to God and God came close to Moses. I think they put their thoughts together to open the river up and let everyone through to the Land of Promises.

Beth: When the water rolled up.

Victoria: When all the slaves were free.

I wonder if we could leave anything out and still have all the story we need?

Jordan: Where the eldest child dies.

Philip: The beginning bit in the desert.

Isla: I think we should leave it all in.

Isobel: The army.

I wonder where you are in the story? Which part of the story is most about you? If you could be

a person or character in the story who would you be?

Connor: I helped Moses. I hugged him. I liked him.

Emily: I was one of the people crossing. I skipped through the water.

Sophie: I danced when I was safe on the other side.

Ben: I ran through the Red Sea. I was happy at the end.

Kyle: Thank God for giving us hope.

Ella: If I was one of them children I would have done somersaults and said yippee!...I was really glad that God made a path through the water to the island.

Kristian: As a slave I would help God do things. I would give water and carry children on my shoulders if I was a slave.

Cody: I would do what God wants me to do and he would let me be free.

Another pupil: I would be the boss of all the servants – Pharaoh.

Amelia: I would be absolutely glad and say thank you to God as one of the children who went to freedom.

Organising the lesson

1. Prepare your materials

Arrange tables with art materials before the children come in. These might include a painting table, a collage table, a modelling table (air drying clay or salt dough), books on the subject for children to dip into (such as *The Exodus* by Brian Wildsmith (OUP 1999, ISBN 0192723979)), computers set up ready with either a Paint or Word program available and some pastel crayons.

2. Prepare your TAs or volunteer helpers (if you have such a luxury!)

Ask adults to scribe the answers that the children make in response to the 'wondering' questions. This will be a helpful benchmark for assessment.

3. Prepare yourself

Familiarise yourself with the faith story – in this case the Exodus story. You can find it in Exodus 1 verses 1–15, and verse 21. A good children's version of the story can be found in 'The Great Escape' in *The Lion Storyteller Bible* by Bob Hartman (Lion 2001, ISBN 9-780745-929217).

Familiarise yourself with the Godly Play script for the story. The script, manual hand movements and notes on materials needed can be found in *The Complete Guide to Godly Play Volume Two* by Jerome W Berryman (BRF 2003, ISBN 1889108-96-0).

5-7

Tasting the story

I always find that food helps the brain! Food is very important in RE lessons too! I pass round the basket of matzos, encouraging children to remember the dry desert as they eat a small part of the matzos. Remind them of the unleavened bread that the People of God had to eat in a hurry as they prepared for their long journey. As they eat, help them to think about what model, painting or picture they might do about their favourite part of the story, or the most important bit, or their part in the story. Ask who has a good idea to start them thinking in the right direction.

The creative work

It's here that the work really begins. Affirm all the work the children produce. One or two might like to talk about their work at the end of the lesson.

The Feast

In one sense, the Feast has already happened in the sharing of the matzos. You could pass round the raisins now.

The sending out

Before the children leave, establish if the work will be displayed in class, be part of a bigger display in school or if the children may take their work home.

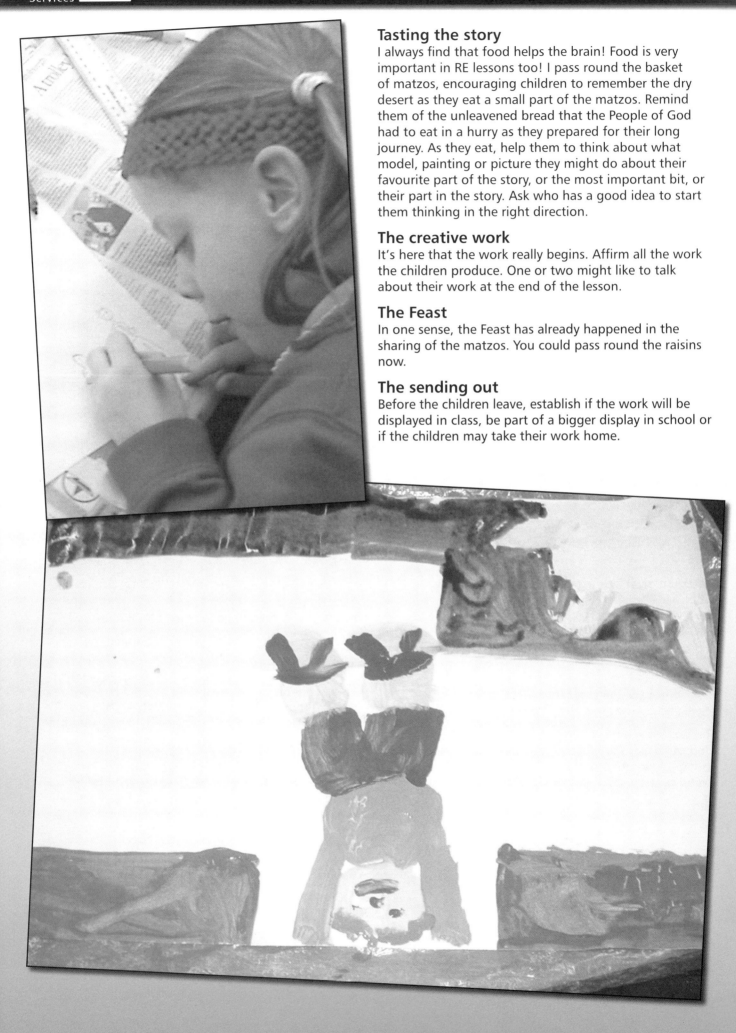

After the lesson

Why not use the children's responses, paintings and models as part of a staff meeting on RE and Assessment?

At Wolston St Margaret's Primary School we found that all the children were operating at least at Level 2. They were using religious words and phrases to identify some features of the story of the Exodus and its importance. You can see from their comments that they were responding sensitively to questions about their own and others' experiences and feelings. Some of the children showed signs of Level 3 as they began to identify the impact that religion has on people's lives (AT1) and go on to make links between their own and other's experiences (AT2). One or two children could even go on to suggest something of Level 4 Attainment Target 2 .They were beginning to describe what influences themselves and others by placing themselves in the Exodus.

In listening to the voice of young children we can learn so much! The Godly Play strategy is an effective way of enabling children to 'speak out'. The activity of telling a religious story using three-dimensional materials engages the children. The use of structured open questions and an opportunity to respond creatively encourages them to participate. The range of follow-up activities allows children to decide for themselves how they want to express their learning, and so is suited to their own learning style.

The teachers felt encouraged and inspired by the quality of the work produced and about how they could use this to help them assess and plan effectively for the next stage of the children's spiritual development.

Engaging with 'big' questions! Some practical activities for 7–11-year-olds

Activity

Life is full of puzzles. Challenge pupils in groups to come up with some really puzzling questions.

The grid below is one structure that is very effective in getting pupils thinking. It is based on a construction known as a Johari Window. Pupils complete it privately before moving into paired/ group discussion.

- In the top right-hand square write down four things which you know about and which other people also know.

- In the bottom right-hand square, list four things you know but which others do not know. These things might be very private. You might prefer to just think about them and not write them down here.

- In the top left-hand square list four things other people know, but you do not know.

- Finally, in the bottom left-hand square write down four things which are unknown to you and others.

For the teacher

Older primary pupils should be given opportunities to

- discuss religious and philosophical questions, giving reasons for their own beliefs and those of others

- reflect on their own and others' insights into life

Talk about

- Are there some things in life that we cannot know – that have no agreed answers or solutions?

- What sorts of questions have you in the bottom left-hand box? How are these puzzling or mysterious?

- How might a Christian, Jew, Muslim, answer some of these questions?

Unknown to me	Known to me
Known to others	Known to others
Unknown to me	Known to me
Unknown to others	Unknown to others

See also

Some other structures to get pupils devising questions include:

- **Guided visualisation**
  e.g. 'Visit to a wise person' in R. Rivett (ed.) *Reflections* (RE Today 2004, ISBN 1-904024-07-6), p.52.

- **Hot seating:**
  for example 'If you had God in the hot seat, what questions would you ask?' (See p.17.)

- **Community of enquiry:** an approach to question generation. (One example can be found on pp.18-20.)

Hot Seat

One member of the group sits centrally and can be asked any question from the floor which they answer from the perspective of a specified role. Teachers and other adults can be in the Hot Seat, answering in role or for themselves. Pupils should *not* be required to answer for themselves.

For example...

- **A visitor:** In the hot seat 'for real'. Pupils prepare questions in advance.

- **Questioning a character:** A pupil takes the role of a character studied, for example Martin Luther King, Mahatma Gandhi, a disciple of Jesus, e.g. Peter or Judas. With younger pupils this can conclude a unit of work, pupils working together to work out questions to ask and answers to give if they are in the 'hot seat'. With older pupils this activity follows careful preparation – pupils may submit questions to the person in the hot seat (and his or her group of advisers) in advance so that they may do some research. Pupils' questions must arise from their own research.

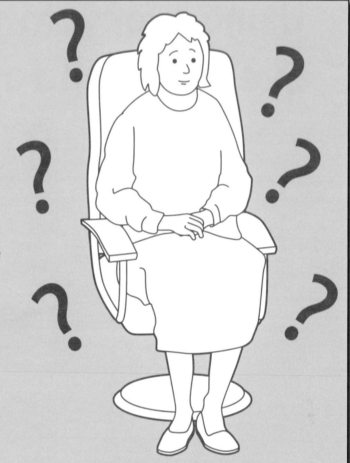

7-11

Question box

Each pupil prepares a thoughtful, open question on a topic. The questions are collected into a box. Children draw out two or three questions, select one and work with others to suggest some answers.

For example...

7-year-olds: Suggest some questions that you would like to ask someone featured in a video clip (e.g. a Hindu worshipping at a home shrine) or a character in a faith story.

10-year-olds: Suggest some questions that puzzle you about, for example, life and death; creation stories.

Circle within a circle discussion

Children's questions can also be used for a 'circle within a circle' discussion. This works well with the 'Big' questions which can arise in RE – those questions for which there are no agreed answers.

- Pupils on the inside pick out one question each; pupils in the outer circle rotate. The pupil on the inner circle asks the same question to each partner, noting down opinions.

- Outer and inner circles swap roles halfway through the activity.

- In pairs, pupils note down main responses to one question and feed back to the group.

See also

For these and other strategies for stimulating questioning: J. Mackley and P. Draycott, *A-Z Practical Learning Strategies for Spiritual and Moral Development* (RE Today 2004, ISBN 1-904024-55-6).

Primary National Strategy, *Creating a Learning Culture: Conditions for Learning* (DfES, 0523-2004 G), p.71.

Using story to stimulate questions and responses

For the teacher

Story is a powerful medium for learners of any age, but a story can be accepted (or rejected) without giving it any further thought. Often, when a story is told in schools, it is followed by the teacher asking questions to ensure pupils have listened and understood: questions such as 'What happened?' 'Who was the main character?' 'What is the message in the story?'

But asking questions should not just be confined to the teacher. Strategies need to be used to encourage the pupils to ask questions as well. The activity in this section, which uses 'Community of Enquiry', a thinking skills strategy, is designed to do just that.

The **objectives** for this lesson for **7–9-year-olds** are:

- to determine what can be learnt about Jesus from the miracle story of Jairus's daughter;

- to develop pupils' skills of interpretation, analysis and reflection;

- to develop pupils' ability to listen to and respond to others' ideas and opinions in a disciplined way.

In **preparation** for the activity, it is important to establish with pupils what you are going to do and what will be expected of them. Starter questions will establish what pupils know and set the scene for the story. The starter questions could focus on who Jesus was, why he is special to Christians and where stories about him can be found.

About 'Community of Enquiry'

This strategy promotes pupils' *philosophical enquiry* and was first developed for classroom use by Matthew Lipman, an American philosopher. It depends upon pupils reading or listening to a narrative (this can also work well with visual images) and asking questions about what they read or hear.

The strategy helps pupils to engage with, interpret, analyse and reflect on a story. The following structure for a 'Community of Enquiry' approach can be varied slightly:

- Listen to the story.

- Pupils generate questions they would like to ask relating to what they have heard. These questions are written up on a whiteboard.

- In pairs/groups, the questions are carefully considered and one question is selected to be discussed by the whole class. Pupils are encouraged to justify or give reasons why they have selected that particular question.

- As a whole class, discuss the chosen questions for each pair/group, with the view of selecting only one question for class discussion. Encouraging a structured response to comments by pupils beginning with 'I agree (or disagree) with ... because....' helps pupils to listen and think carefully about what other people are saying.

Being involved in pair/group/class discussions and listening to the opinions and ideas of their peers helps pupils to:

- develop their own reasoning and thinking;

- assess the quality of their questioning (are these the best questions to ask and why?);

- identify and distinguish between important and trivial questions;

- rise to the challenge of answering the questions themselves;

- arrive at group consensus or conclusions.

RE Today web link: an adapted version of the story of Jairus's daughter suitable for 7–9-year-olds is available to subscribers on the RE Today website: www.retoday.org.uk.

The story of Jairus's daughter – raising questions

Activity

7-9

- Retell the story (Mark 5.21-24, 35-43) or use the version that can be found on the RE Today website.

- Ask the pupils what questions they would like to ask. These are written/ typed up on a flipchart or whiteboard. (The class who trialled this activity posed the questions which appear at the bottom of the page.)

- In groups, pupils discuss the questions and choose one they would like to explore further, identifying the reasons why they are choosing this question.

- The teacher writes the chosen questions on the board. (The questions chosen by the class trialling the activity are the questions highlighted below.)

- Pupils discuss which question is the most interesting, important or or puzzling. Pupils from the group who proposed the questions have to explain why the question was chosen. Others join in the discussion with 'I agree (or disagree) with ... because....'

A class vote decides which is selected and the question is discussed.

To start this off, the pupils who proposed the question explain their thoughts, with the rest of the class being encouraged to join in. Discussion may be structured with 'I agree' or 'I don't agree' statements. (The question chosen by the class was 'How do we know about the story of Jairus's daughter if Jesus told everyone not to say anything?')

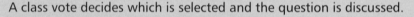

The Story of Jairus's daughter
Some questions children asked

- How do we know about the story of Jairus's daughter if Jesus told everyone not to say anything?

- How did Jesus bring Jairus's daughter back to life?

- What was Jairus's daughter called?

- How long did she live afterwards?

- When did this happen?

- How old was Jesus?

- What was her illness/ why did she become ill / was she born with the illness?

- How long had she been ill?

- How long was Jesus away for?

- How did Jesus get across the lake?

- How many people were in the crowd?

- How did Jesus know she was only asleep and not dead?

- Why did Jesus not want them to tell anyone?

- Why did Jesus choose to go with Jairus and not anyone else?

- How do we know Jairus's name when we don't know the names of many other people he helped?

What to do next.....

Answering the question: Some questions raised by pupils may be difficult or impossible to answer and therefore suggestions as to the possible answer will be raised by pupils. In the class which trialled this activity it was possible for the teacher to answer the question after the pupils suggested that someone must have told others what had happened, and that the story was passed on in order for it to be written down. As pupils wanted to know more, the teacher explained that the author of Mark's Gospel was possibly a follower of Peter, who was present at the event according to the Gospels.

Debriefing: Summarise, through questioning and answering, what pupils have learnt (or what knowledge has been reinforced) about Jesus. Talk about questions raised which were difficult to answer.

Ask pupils to identify what they can do better as a result of the lesson ('listen to each other'; 'take turns to talk'; 'think more about the story' – speaking and listening skills and skills of interpretation, analysis and reflection).

What did the pupils learn about Jesus?

As some previous work had focused on miracles, many of the pupils simply 'accepted' the miracle in this story. They felt that the story did not tell them anything new about Jesus but in both the group and class discussions the teacher observed that pupils knew Jesus

- was popular with the people
- was known by a lot of different people
- travelled to different places
- had special friends whom he trusted (Peter, James and John)
- was able to perform miracles
- was kind and caring.

What did the pupils think and feel about the activity?

- I liked it!
- I enjoyed the story.
- I liked talking about the story with my friends.

'I can' statements useful for setting targets/assessment tasks

Level 2

I can talk about what I have learnt about Jesus from the story of Jairus's daughter. (AT1)

I can ask some good questions about this story. (AT2)

Level 3

I can make a link between the story of Jairus's daughter and other stories I have heard about Jesus. (AT1)

I can ask important questions about this story and suggest answers, making links between what I and others think about the story of Jairus's daughter. (AT2)

Teacher's comments on the activity

It was important not to dismiss any questions that pupils came up with, but that they were challenged to explain why their questions were important. For example, 'What was Jairus's daughter called?' might seem irrelevant but the pupil revealed that if they knew her name they might be able to find out if she appeared in other stories about Jesus and what happened to her.

This particular class had heard some miracle stories previously and were able to give reasoned explanations of what a miracle is. This concept would probably be the focus of the questions for pupils who were hearing a miracle story for the first time. Older pupils would be more likely to question the possibility of miracles.

This was the first time the pupils had encountered the 'Community of Enquiry' approach and without exception they responded well, but next time they will need to be challenged to think more carefully about the questions they want to ask immediately after listening to the story.

Using digital resources in RE – and creating your own

For the teacher

'Keyhole movies' and 'morph sequences' are two types of digital resource that can be used effectively to support and sharpen pupils' ability to **think speculatively** and **observe closely** – important skills to support progression in RE.

Such resources can occasionally be found on the internet, but can also be easily developed by teachers and pupils themselves. They are ideal for use with whiteboard technologies, and can also be used independently of these.

The two activities outlined here relate to Sikhism but can be used in a range of faith contexts and in a variety of ways, e.g.:

- **preparing** pupils to visit a place of worship, or welcome a visitor from a local faith community into the RE classroom;

- **encouraging** respectful and purposeful questioning, reflection and dialogue;

- **bringing authentic resources** from a faith community into the classroom, particularly valuable when studying a faith community that is not represented locally;

- **providing a stimulus** to creating your own digital video resource based on a faith community local to the school.

The activities also support the QCA's non-statutory National Framework for RE (2004) in England by stimulating the provision of opportunities for pupils to encounter religion through visitors and visits to places of worship and developing the use of ICT.

CLEO - www.cleo.net.uk

Time Morph – CLEO's free downloadable tool

7-11

See also

- **CLEO** (www.cleo.net.uk)

Check out CLEO for its growing collection of free, high-quality digital video resources for RE, for all key stages. Resources that focus on Sikhism on this website include:

- **Sukh Aasan**: Taking the Sri Guru Granth Sahib to 'Sach Khand', the nightly resting place;

- **Keyhole Movie 1**: Karah Parshad;

- **Keyhole Movie 2**: Carrying the Sri Guru Granth Sahib to Sach Khand;

- **Beliefs and questions**: Sikhism.

Acknowledgements

We are very grateful to the following for giving us permission to film inside the Gurdwara, and for supporting our project to develop digital resources to enhance learning about and from Sikhism.

- **Dr Parvinder Singh Garcha**, General Secretary, Sri Guru Singh Sabha, Southall;

- **The Congregation** (Sangat) and the **Executive Committee** of Gurdwara Sri Guru Singh Sabha, Southall;

- **Mr Ajit Singh Singhota**.

We are also indebted to **Roger Lang** of CLEO, who undertook the filming, editing, and developing of the digital resources.

RE Today web link: Detailed instructions on how to create morph sequences and keyhole movies with CLEO's Time Morph tool and Macromedia Flash MX 2004 are available to subscribers on the RE Today.

Preparing to visit a gurdwara – using a keyhole movie

For the teacher

'**Through the keyhole – 2 & 3'** are 'keyhole movie' resources on the CLEO web site [www.cleo.net.uk/resources/index.php?ks=2&cur=15]. They were filmed in the Gurdwara Sri Guru Singh Sabha, Havelock Road, Southall.

- **Movie 2**: Karah Parshad.

- **Movie 3**: Procession – the Granthi carrying the Sri Guru Granth Sahib very respectfully to 'Sach Khand', its nightly resting place.

As a starter, these two resources can be used to:

- encourage pupils to focus on detail (visual and audio) to draw out / infer meaning;

- engage pupils in wanting to 'solve the puzzle';

- provide a stimulus to a challenging question, such as: 'If a person was blind or deaf, would it be possible for them to worship?';

- prepare pupils for a visit to a gurdwara or to receive a visitor from the local Sikh community.

Making your own keyhole movies

If you have an interactive whiteboard, try using the '**keyhole**' or '**spotlight**' tool. If you have **Macromedia Flash MX 2004**, then check out RE Today's website for instructions (www.retoday.org.uk) – all you need are some digital footage and 15 minutes!

Preparing the Sri Guru Granth Sahib for its nightly rest

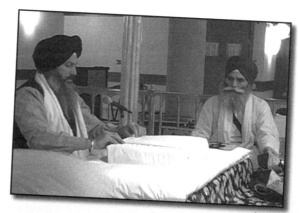

Worshippers watch as the Sri Guru Granth Sahib is placed in 'Sach Khand', an upstairs room for its nightly rest

Activity 1 Keyhole movie

Activity

- **Ask pupils to:**

  - **talk about** a visit to someone's home – perhaps grandparents, or a friend in a different country;

  - **work in pairs** to choose and list four things in their own houses which they feel identify themselves and their family.

- **Introduce the 'keyhole movie':**

  - **explain** that it is a 'keyhole view' into a place that is special to someone;

  - **ask** pupils to suggest whom it is special to, and why;

  - **slowly move the 'keyhole'** around the screen (teacher or pupils can do this), inviting pupils to suggest ideas. Prompt questions could include:

    - What do you see? What do you hear?

    - How does the movie make you feel? What might it remind you of?

    - What do the colours and shapes tell you?

- **When the movie has been identified, ask pupils:**

  - What do you think will happen next?

  - What else do we need to find out to help us understand what is so special about this place for Sikhs? Where can we look to find out?

  - What three questions would you like to ask the Granthi?

For the teacher

'Church time morph' is a morph sequence on the CLEO website (www.cleo.net.uk/resources/index.php?ks=3&cur=15) showing two photographs of St Thomas's Church, Lancaster, taken 50 years apart. Clicking on the right button of the mouse allows you to zoom in or out.

A short morphing sequence has the capacity to:

- **convey a complex idea** using a visual vocabulary that is part of the pupils' culture. The concept of bodily transformation, as well as being an ancient and widespread theme in traditional narratives, frequently features in cartoons and science fiction;

- **present concepts and ideas in a variety of ways** which increases the chance of them being understood and remembered.

As a starter this resource can be used to explore the concept of 'continuity and change' in the context of local religious expression and worship – that while some things remain constant (e.g. belief in God), other things change (e.g.style of worship).

CLEO's Time Morph tool

Developing your own morphing sequences is easy! Try using CLEO's own **Time Morph tool**, available for free download from www.cleo.net. uk/resources/index.php?ks=2&cur=15. If you have **Macromedia Flash MX 2004**, then check out RE Today's website for instructions (www. retoday.org.uk) – all you need are two suitable digital images and 15 minutes!

St Thomas's Church, Lancaster - fifty years ago

7-11

St Thomas's Church, Lancaster - as it is today
www.st.tees.org.uk

Activity 2 Church timemorph

Activity

Open the morph sequence (it operates on a loop) and ask pupils to:

- work in pairs to **note down the differences** they observe;

- move into fours to **share ideas**, and add to/amend ideas as appropriate;

- **feed back** ideas to the whole class (key points recorded by teacher on the board);

- work in fours to **categorise** the key points into the following groups:
  - building
  - worship
  - people
  - feelings

- **identify reasons** for the changes they observe;

- **identify three things** they want to investigate when they visit their local church;

- **identify three questions** they would like to ask the priest/minister.

Using poetry to stimulate and express children's BIG questions

I wonder...

RE's obsession with puzzling questions is fertile ground for poetic imagination. Where are we from? Where are we going? What are we worth? What's it all for? All the questions and all the replies are the territory for this theme.

Here we suggest one strategy you might like to try with your pupils to get them thinking about what puzzles them or makes them wonder. It incorporates opportunities for reflection and expression – two key skills related to learning from religion.

Reflect and express – using images and poetry to reflect on puzzling questions

Objective: To encourage pupils'

• reflection on 'puzzling' questions which make them wonder and

• creative expression of their own big questions in the form of a poem.

Resources: Images of the natural world and the universe (from the internet) to aid reflection and to stimulate puzzling questions. Poem displayed on whiteboard.

Procedure
5-minute starter: **Mystery object** on screen (e.g. close-up of flower/insect).

See also

Stilling exercise: details can be found in J. Mackley and P. Draycott (eds) *A–Z Practical Learning Strategies*, pp.59-61, published by RE Today 2004, ISBN 1-904024-55-6.

• Whilst looking at the mystery object, ask pupils to think of five questions, each beginning with one of the following words: who, what, where, how, why.

• After briefly sharing children's questions, ask them to suggest which of these types of questions might be the most puzzling. Use this to get children thinking about 'Why?' questions.

• Explain that the lesson will give pupils an opportunity to reflect (have a time of stillness to ponder/think with care) on some big questions about the world and life that make them wonder. They will then express their ideas in the form of a poem, drawing on skills learnt in literacy lessons.

Stilling and reflection

• Do a stilling exercise to settle children, to help them reflect.

• Display the question key words: WHO WHAT WHERE HOW WHY.

• Show children a range of images of the natural world using PowerPoint. Ask them to notice what they wonder about as they watch.

Recording questions

- Give pupils a few m oments to record their thoughts, using the sentence starter 'I wonder...'. They could do this as a mind map, or use 'I wonder...' as a sentence stem.

Expressing ideas

- Put the following poem/s on the screen. Pupils listen to the poem/s and identify any of their own questions that are similar to or different from those in Sophia or Kennedy's poems.

- Talk about whether there are some 'big' questions that all people ask – and consider whether these sorts of questions can easily be answered.

- Explain how these are the questions religions try to answer – and answers are often linked to what people believe.

Creative expression: writing a poem

Using poetry writing frames and structures explored in Literacy, pupils write their own poem on the theme 'I wonder...'.

Some may wish to share this with the class on completion.

I Wonder

I wonder how the world was made.
I wonder why the sky is blue.
I wonder if the world's got bigger.
I wonder if God pulls a trigger
To change from light to dark.
Does he have a magic spark?

I wonder if God sees
Every person in the world.
Every boy and every girl.
If so, how?
Can he see us now?
I've been asking these questions
For days and days.
My mind is in
A question maze.

I wonder why nobody knows.
I wonder why nobody goes
To find the reply
To my question "Why?"

Sophia Brousas, aged 9
Acton Park Junior School

9–11

Why do the stars come out?
Why do we have names?
How far does the sea go?
How does the moon shine?

Why does a wasp sting?
Why is the grass green?
Why can't we fly?
Why are the clouds in the sky?

Kennedy Lamming, aged 6
Parkwood Infants School, Scunthorpe

Extension activity: The Biggest Question of Them All

Ask pupils to come up with as many 'WHY? questions as they can. Ask them to sort these into different groups; they can decide the groupings. Decide which is the 'biggest question of them all'.

Display this key question – and other questions. Refer back to it in your RE lessons. See if you can find out how people from each religion you study might respond to it.

Some other themes to get children thinking

Life's like... invite pupils to look at life from any angle they like, making metaphors and symbols. Is life like a puzzle? a journey? a rat race? a disease? a gift?

Where is God? Atheists say God is nowhere. Agnostics think he may be hiding. Feminists think he's a she. Believers may place the divine in the human heart, in the sacred space, in the running waves or in deep space. Poetry around this theme encourages reflections from all points of view.

Faith: Noah trusted the promise of the rainbow. Prophet Muhammad ﷺ trusted the voice of Angel Jibril. Whom do you trust? Where do you put your faith? Invite pupils to reflect on their own issues and ideas about trust and faith – in God, or in humanity.

These themes featured in the PCfRE Spirited Poetry competition 2005.

I can...

The following pupil-friendly criteria could be used to assess children's responses to this activity.

To what extent *can pupils:*

- create a reflective poem on the puzzling questions I think about when looking at the natural world and the stars (L3 / AT2);

- create a poem expressing my questions about creation and God, referring to ideas from religions I have studied (L4 / AT2);

- make a link between a big question I have raised and what a religion I have studied says about this (L3 / AT1);

- link up some religious beliefs and some religious responses to some 'why ' questions about creation and the natural world (L4 / AT1).

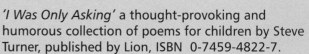

See also

For more examples of children's Spirited Poetry see the publication of this name by Lat Blaylock, published by RMEP 2006, ISBN 1851753494.

'I Was Only Asking' a thought-provoking and humorous collection of poems for children by Steve Turner, published by Lion, ISBN 0-7459-4822-7.

Beliefs and questions: Where do we come from? Where do we go?

For the teacher

These lesson ideas aim to help your pupils in the 9–11 age range learn from Hindu ideas about some important beliefs and questions through some well-thought-out practical classroom learning activities. The lessons deal with questions of origin (Who am I? Where do we come from?) and questions of destiny (What is the point of life? What happens when we die?). Using Hindu story and simple illustrations, pupils think for themselves about these big questions. The work on pages 29 and 30 is mostly about teasing ideas out of stories, looking for meaning. Pages 31 and 32 deal more with creative expression of the pupils' own ideas and beliefs.

See also

Authentic Hindu materials: The International Society for Krishna Consciousness provides artefacts, visual materials and educational ideas: ISKCON Educational Services, Dharam Marg, Hillfield Lane, Aldenham, Herts WD25 8EZ. Email: ies@pamho. net Tel: 01923 859 578.

9–11

Information file

Hindu traditions are very diverse: never start a sentence with the words 'All Hindus…'. This work uses some mainstream stories, but there are many others too. One fairly constant theme of Hindu answers to questions of origins and destiny is that we are part of huge cycles and circular movements. This contrasts with the often linear views of life that Westerners hold. This is worth remembering as you teach the topic, and worth discussing with learners in many different ways.

RE Today web link: Additional materials for learning, based on this article, including a PowerPoint presentation, is available to subscribers on the RE Today website www.retoday.org.uk

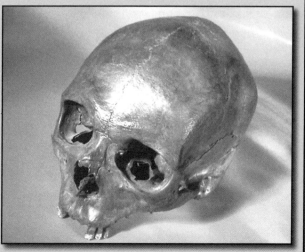

A thinking puzzle: ask pupils which of these pictures comes first. Most will say the pram. Challenge them in pairs to think of as many examples as possible where the skull comes first, and the pram afterwards. This simple thinking challenge opens up the idea that life might not be as 'linear' as we often suppose.

Classroom activities

- **Starter:** Ask pupils to think about seeing. There are some things we cannot see, but would like to. Get them to close their eyes and imagine they are looking into a magic mirror! If they could choose to see one thing from the past, one from the future, one from someone else's mind and one from beyond this universe, what would they choose?

  Ask pupils to write these down. This imaginative activity links with Brahma's four-way sight. In Hindu iconography the divine visionary power is symbolised by the god Brahma's four heads, looking at everything at once.

- **Visual learning:** Give each group of three pupils a copy of page 29 (enlarge it if you can). Ask them to fill in their observations and then their thoughts, in bullet points, as many as they can. The aim is to get them speculating and thinking about some material that may be strange to them. After 10 minutes, get two groups to compare notes and add to their work what they learned from each other. Discuss questions arising from this as a class, bearing in mind that mysteries can't always be solved!

- **Sequencing:** Make enough copies of page 30 for groups of three. Cut them up, and shuffle the set of 12 cards, then ask groups to sequence the story. Give time for this: the activity is deliberately ambiguous, and there is more than one 'right' way to put it together. The aim is for learners to familiarise themselves with the structure and detail of the story. When pupils have finished, ask them to sum up the story in 12 very short sentences, one for each card.

- **Origins and destinies:** Ask pupils to think about the idea of a signpost. When we pass a signpost, it tells us where we came from, and where we are going. These are two important ideas. Give them a big signpost, or get them to draw one: on the arm that points backwards, they should write all the answers they can think of to the question 'Where did I come from?' On the forward-pointing arm, everything that answers the question 'Where are you going?' Multiple answers – including the witty ones – are best. Can anyone think of 10? 15? 20?

- **Comparing:** Set your group of higher achievers the task of comparing this Hindu creation story to one from Judaism (Genesis 1) or another tradition. Ask them to find five similarities and five differences.

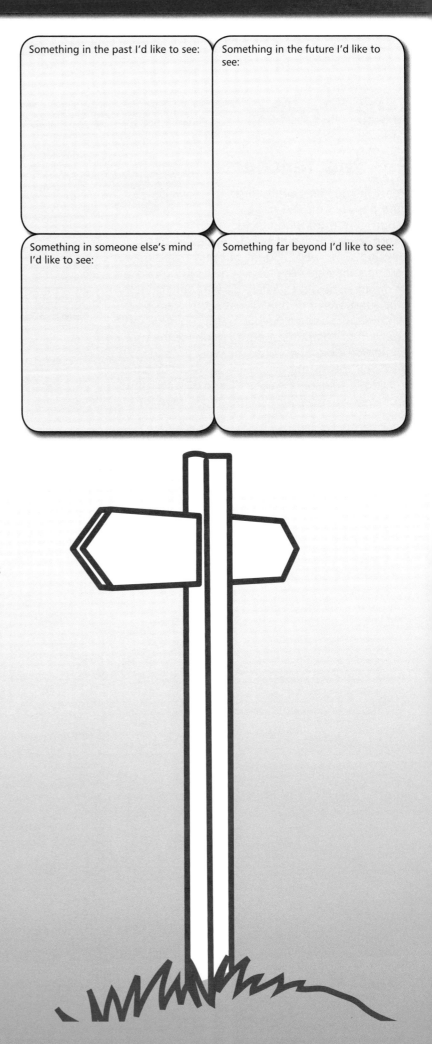

Something in the past I'd like to see:

Something in the future I'd like to see:

Something in someone else's mind I'd like to see:

Something far beyond I'd like to see:

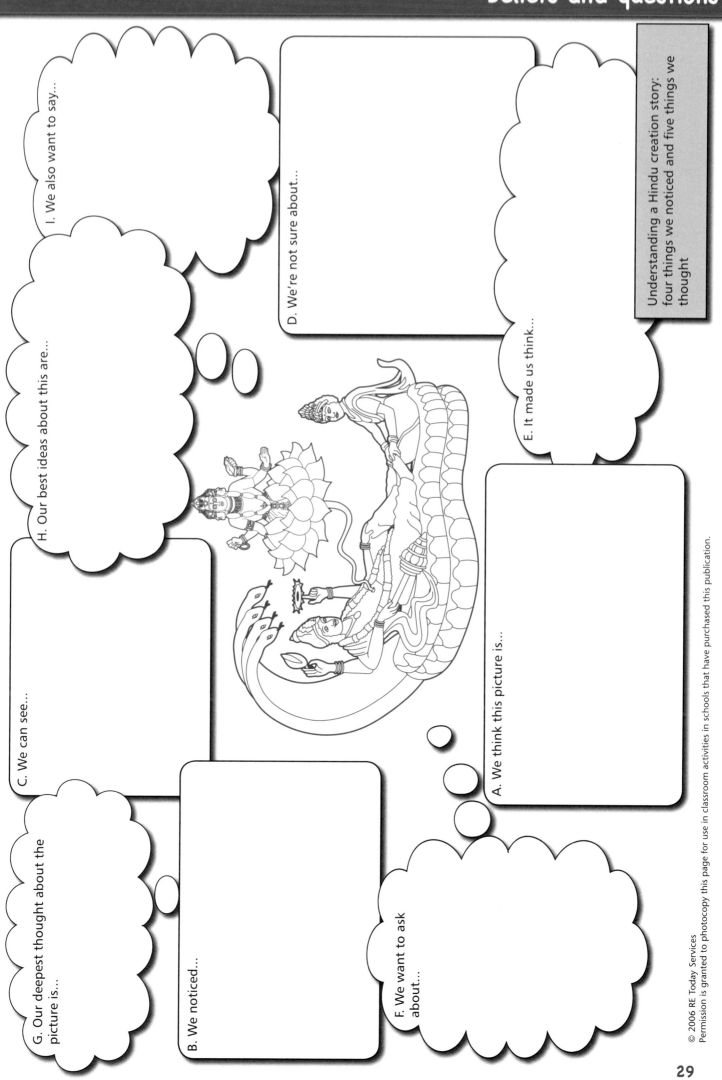

I. We also want to say…

G. Our deepest thought about the picture is…

H. Our best ideas about this are…

D. We're not sure about…

C. We can see…

E. It made us think…

B. We noticed…

A. We think this picture is…

F. We want to ask about…

Understanding a Hindu creation story: four things we noticed and five things we thought

A Hindu creation story told in 12 parts for sequencing

In this story, some of life's biggest questions are answered: Where do we come from? How did we get here? What started everything? There are many answers to this question. The answers here are from Hindu traditions.

As he meditated, **Brahma** saw in his heart an image of another of the gods: it was **Krishna**.

Krishna guided **Brahma** to create living beings.

When the Creator **Brahma** had made the world, there was a job for **Vishnu**: 'I am the preserver' he said. 'I will enter every atom, every creature, and own them all. I will keep them alive.'

Long, long ago, when all of our universe was new, the great god **Vishnu** rested blissfully on a mighty snake in the waters.

So **Brahma** gave life to **Shiva**, and **Shiva** married the goddess **Shakti**, Mother Nature.

From their marriage all living things are born, and come on earth.

And there was a job for **Shiva** too. 'I am the destroyer' he said. 'Every living thing grows and then passes away, so that new life can be born. I will end the old, and bring in the new. I will beat out the rhythm of life.'

The first thing to grow was a flower, a pink and beautiful lotus flower. It grew from the belly button of the great god **Vishnu.**

Next **Brahma** created all the universe we can see – from a vacuum of nothing he made air and fire, water and earth. He created taste and touch, sight, smell and hearing, so that created beings could enjoy the world.

The story has many meanings. It means that our universe began with love, not by an accident. It means we all take part in one life, we all come from the same source.

As the first petals opened, there was a divine being inside: it was the god **Brahma**, with his four heads. He meditated from the centre of the flower. He thought deeply about the mystery of the universe.

Next, **Brahma** made the brilliant sun and the delicate moon, stars and planets, days and nights.

The story doesn't tell us a history or a scientific account of where we come from, but it does tell us that our purpose in life is from the gods and goddesses.

Cut up a copy of this page into 12 cards, one set for each trio of pupils. The correct order reads down the page, column by column.

1	5	9
2	6	10
3	7	11
4	8	12

Hindu Ideas: life's more like a circle than a line

Activities

1. Look carefully at the picture with a partner. What is it about? What does it mean? Make a note of five things you notice and three questions it makes you want to ask.

2. Make some think bubbles and add some feelings words to the picture: how does it feel to be young or old? Think of two different words for each of the stages of life in the picture.

3. Read the paragraph on the right.

4. What do Hindu people mean by reincarnation?

5. What do you think about the mystery of what happens when we die?

6. 'Destiny' is a word a bit like 'destination'. It's about where you're going. In your own life, do you have a destiny? Where do you hope to go in life? And where do you hope to go after death? Create a group collage with pictures and images torn from magazines to show your ideas. Call it 'Our Destinies'.

Where are we going? What do Hindus believe?

If you measured all the chemicals in a person's body just before they died, and then again just afterwards, the body would be the same. But the most important thing – the life – would have gone.

This mysterious fact has puzzled all humans since the ancient times. Some say the 'real you' goes to heaven, or becomes a ghost, or just stops existing altogether. Hindu traditions teach a different destiny. The body is like old clothes, and when it wears out, throw it away. The real you will take new clothes. This is often called **reincarnation**; it means that the real person will return again to the earth in a new body. When one body dies, another is born.

The picture shows this idea of life as a circle. In Hindu teaching, your destiny is to be born again. Hindu tradition also teaches that there is an escape from this cycle of birth and death. This is called **Moksha**.

Assessment outcomes from this work

If a pupil can say 'yes' to some of these, they are able to work at:	I can... statements enable teachers and pupils to understand their progress.
Level 2	• Retell simply a Hindu creation story. • Identify two different answers to the question 'What happens when we die?'
Level 3	• Describe the main point of a Hindu creation story. • Describe a Hindu idea about reincarnation. • Make a simple link between my ideas and questions about life after death and some simple Hindu ideas.
Level 4	• Show that I understand the words 'origin', 'destiny' and 'reincarnation' for myself. • Apply the idea of origins and destiny to my own answers to the questions: Where are we from? Where are we going?'
Level 5	• Explain some similarities and differences between ideas about reincarnation and other ideas about life after death. • Express my own views of religious ideas about origin and destiny, referring to the religions I've studied.

Concluding this work: personal evaluation

This work is conceptually demanding for 10–11s, so the activities and stimuli are relatively simple, enabling engagement with beliefs and questions.

Here are three reflective suggestions that aim to help pupils crystallise their own questions and beliefs. These activities are very well suited to circle time.

Reflections in the group: Sit in a circle and ask pupils to spend 60 seconds thinking quietly about the work. If they could ask 'the one who sees everything' (Brahma?) one question, what would it be? Go round the group, hearing the questions. It would be good to get a classroom assistant to record the questions in writing, or on audio equipment. Teachers are often surprised at the depth and profundity this activity reveals.

Expressing our own beliefs: Remind pupils that in RE we study many beliefs, so we can be clearer about our own. Beliefs about origin and destiny isn't an easy topic, but it's good to speak clearly about it. Invite pupils around the circle to say what they believe about one or both of the questions. Make sure they feel comfortable to 'pass' as well as comfortable to speak.

Creative reflection: Ask pupils to think and talk in pairs in the circle about how to make two symbols, one for their past or origins and one for their future or destiny. Then send them to their own space to make the symbols. No writing is needed – this can be a private piece of work.